THE GET FUZZY EXPERIENCE

Other books by Darby Conley

The Dog Is Not a Toy (House Rule #4)

Fuzzy Logic

Groovitude

THE Get Fuzzy experience

are you Bucksperienced

by
Darby Conley

**Andrews McMeel
Publishing**

Kansas City

Get Fuzzy can be viewed on the Internet at:

www.comics.com/comics/getfuzzy

ATTENTION: SCHOOLS AND BUSINESSES

Andrews McMeel books are available at quantity discounts with bulk purchase for educational, business, or sales promotional use. For information, please write to: Special Sales Department, Andrews McMeel Publishing, 4520 Main Street, Kansas City, Missouri 64111.

To my sister, Caity, and my brother, Tim

MREOWW

WE WERE IN THE PARK AND HE STARTED SCREAMING THAT HE'D LOST SMACKY.

WHERE WERE YOU WHEN YOU LOST HIM, BUCK?

AS I WAS GETTING KICKED OUT OF THE SANDBOX, I REALIZED THAT I DIDN'T HAVE SMACKY AND I...I COULDN'T SEE SATCHEL ...I LOST SMACKY... AND I LOST MY BEST FRIEND...

I'M HERE NOW...

I'M TALKIN' ABOUT SMACKY!

OK, SO YOU DON'T REMEMBER WHERE YOU LAST HAD SMACKY. *CALM DOWN*, WE'LL SEE IF WE CAN JAR YOUR MEMORY BY USING A LITTLE WORD ASSOCIATION—NOW, SAY THE FIRST WORD THAT POPS INTO YOUR HEAD AS I SAY THINGS.

PLAYGROUND.

PLAYGROUND.

TRASH CAN

TRASH CAN.

SANDBOX.

SANDBOX.

THAT WAS EASY. SO WHERE IS SMACKY?

ALRIGHT... LET ME EXPLAIN THIS A BIT MORE.

GUYS! I FOUND SMACKY!

HE WAS BURIED IN THE SAND BOX, BUT I SMELLED HIM AND DUG HIM OUT!

WELL, A HAPPY ENDING FOR ONCE. SAY "*THANKS*" TO SATCHEL FOR FINDING HIM, BUCK.

BUT SMACKY'S NOT LOST, HE'S RIGHT HERE...

sprouts athens, ga.

OH, NOT THIS AGAIN, *BETTER LIVING THROUGH DENIAL*, EH, BUCK?

YOU BETTER BELIEVE IT.

sprouts athens, ga.

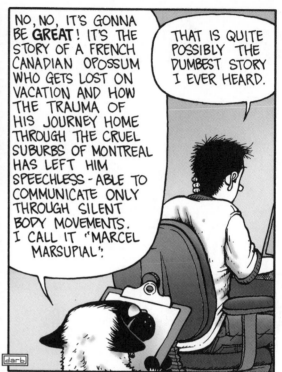

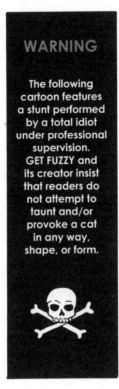

16

17

BUCKY, THIS LETTER IS A SCAM. THEY'RE JUST TRYING TO SUCKER YOU INTO BUYING $200-RAFFLE TICKETS.

DON'T WORRY ABOUT **ME**, ROBBO, I WASN'T BORN YESTERDAY.

SOMETIMES I WONDER...

HEY, I CAN REMEMBER BACK A GOOD 3 OR 4 DAYS **AT LEAST**... IN FACT, YESTERDAY IS PARTICULARLY VIVID, AND **NO BIRTH**.

SO... YOU RIPPED MY BRIEFCASE OPEN LOOKING FOR A CREDIT CARD TO BUY RAFFLE TICKETS AFTER I TOLD YOU **NOT** TO BUY THEM... WHAT PART OF "DON'T BUY RAFFLE TICKETS" DO YOU NOT UNDERSTAND?

I PREFER NOT TO ANSWER THAT.

I KNOW! **I** KNOW! IT'S THE **FIRST** PART, RIGHT?

OK. THAT TAKES CARE OF THAT. BUCKY, YOUR NAME IS OFFICIALLY BARRED FROM THE RAFFLE DRAWING AT THE CATNIP PALACE.

BOOP

NUTS.

LIFE IS TOUGH, BUCK. YOU COULDN'T EVEN HAVE GONE TO CLAIM YOUR PRIZE IF YOU **HAD** WON, YOU KNOW.

OH, I WOULD HAVE FIGURED SOMETHING OUT. LIKE THEY SAY: *WHEN LIFE GIVES YOU LEMONS, CHUCK 'EM AT DOGS.*

I DON'T LIKE "THEM."

23

I CAN'T BELIEVE I'M LETTING BUCKY HAVE AN "ANT FARM"...

WELL...MAYBE WE COULD THINK OF IT AS PRACTICE FOR WHEN HE BECOMES A MOTHER.

SATCHEL...THAT MAKES NO—

I KNOW THAT, I JUST THOUGHT IT MIGHT HELP IF WE *PRETEND* THAT!

BUCKY, ARE... ARE YOU EATING AN *ANT*?!

MM-HM.

AW, *BUCKY!* IS *THAT* WHY YOU WANTED AN "ANT FARM"? TO BE YOUR OWN, PERSONAL *VENDING MACHINE*?!

RELAX, ROBBO. IT'S A WILD HOUSE ANT.

SO... YOU'RE SAYIN' YOU ONLY EAT *FREE-RANGE* ANTS.

THAT'S CORRECT.

HEY, SATCH, DID YOU SEE THE PRESENT MY MOM SENT YOU?

YEAH, THEY WERE GOOD!

WHAT DO YOU MEAN THEY WERE "GOOD"?

THOSE MUFFIN THINGS. I ATE 'EM.

DUDE, THOSE WERE FLOWER BULBS. THEY WEREN'T MUFFINS, THEY WERE *DIRT*.

OH. WELL, BUCKY WOULD HAVE EATEN THEM WHEN THEY BLOOMED, ANYWAY.

YOU GOT THAT RIGHT, BULB EATER.

MAN, THIS VEGGIE CHILI S—

WATCH IT... THIS IS MY MOM'S RECIPE...

THIS VEGGIE CHILI... UM... DOES WHAT A HOOVER DOES...

GO TO YOUR CLOSET.

THIS CHILI RUNS THE FBI?

SO BY THE END OF THE WEEK, IT WAS DOWN OVER NINE POINTS. IT **SO** DEVALUED MY PORTFOLIO.

YOU SHOULD **SO** CONSIDER LIQUI-DATING SOME OF YOUR ASSETS AND MOVING THEM TO HIGHER YIELDING VENTURES.

I AM **SO** NOT TOUCHING ANY ASSETS UNTIL THE NEXT QUARTER.

WELL, *OBVIOUSLY* I'M NOT SUGGESTING YOU—

MY ASSETS ARE IN TUNA.

EXCUSE ME?

UM... WHO ARE YOU?

I'M BUCKY.

28

HA HA! GOT MILK?

SHUT UP.

THANKS FOR HANGING OUT WITH THE GUYZOS TONIGHT, JOE. THEY'RE FINE DURING THE DAY, BUT THEY DO FREAK OUT ALONE AT NIGHT.

ARE YOU KIDDING? I LOVE COMING HERE. IT'S LIKE A SITCOM. YOU GUYS ARE LIKE "DIFF'RENT SPECIES."

WELL, WE CERTAINLY HAVE THE MESSED-UP-CHILD-ACTOR THING GOIN' ON.

WHAT'CHOO TALKIN' 'BOUT WILCO?!

MMM. THAT SMELLS GOOD...WHAT IS IT?

WELL, I KNOW THAT ROB IS A VEGETARIAN, SO I THOUGHT I'D MAKE YOU GUYS SOMETHING SPECIAL—IT'S JERK CHICKEN.

HEY, WHAT CHICKEN ISN'T?

A.C.R.O.N.Y.M.

30

31

35

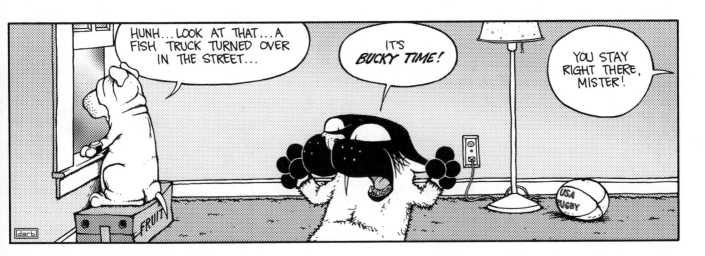

38

Artist's suggestion: **HUG A VET.**

43

YOU... YOU SMELL LIKE THE *FERRET.*

NO, I DON'T. RELAX.

YOU SMELL LIKE MR. SQUIGGLY! I DEMAND TO KNOW WHAT YOU'VE BEEN DOING!

I HAVEN'T BEEN DOING ANYTHING, CHILL OUT!

LISTEN, DON'T TRY TO PLAY DUMB WITH *ME,* I'M THE *KING* OF D-WAIT... THAT'S NOT GONNA COME OUT RIGHT...

HEY, BUCK, WE'RE RE-READING *HARRY POTTER,* WANNA COME LISTEN? WE'RE ON THE TROLL PART.

I DON'T LIKE TROLLS...

ROB, I THINK I'M A LITTLE TOO SOPHISTICATED FOR *"STORY TIME."*

E TROL AIRS AN A SLYTH

OOO, DID YOU HEAR THAT, SMACKY? A BIG, UGLY, NASTY, *TROLL!*

PLEASE TELL ME YOU'RE NOT WAITING BY THE DOOR FOR THE FERRET TO COME DOWN THE HALLWAY...

SORRY, ROB, I CAN'T DO THAT.

MAN, WHAT IS YOUR PROBLEM WITH THAT FERRET? WHO ARE YOU, *RUDY GIULIANI?!* JUST LEAVE THE WEASEL ALONE!

SORRY, ROB, I CAN'T DO THAT.

YEAH, HE'S *RUDE*-Y!

45

47

AW, LOOK AT THIS...SILLY YELLOW JOURNALISM...

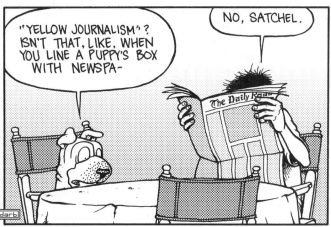

"YELLOW JOURNALISM"? ISN'T THAT, LIKE, WHEN YOU LINE A PUPPY'S BOX WITH NEWSPA-

NO, SATCHEL.

AND AS THE LEAD SLED TEAM COMES INTO VIEW, IT'S -- CAN IT *BE*?!? *YES!* IT'S THE TEAM LED BY THE ROOKIE *SATCHEL POOCH!* HIS HUGE MUSCLES ARE STRAINING AS HE PULLS THE REST OF HIS TIRED TEAM TOWARD THE FINISH LINE!!

THE CROWD IS GOING WILD! HE'S ABOUT TO WIN THE 1,100 MILE-LONG IDITAROD! JUST WHO *IS* THIS INCREDIBLE DOG WHO'S COME OUT OF NOWHERE TO LEAD HIS RAGGED TEAM TO...TO, UM...

...HI.

MUSH!

SWOOSH

SOME PEOPLE ARE PASSIVE-AGGRESSIVE, BUCKY IS PASS*ING*-AGGRESSIVE...

MAN...

BUCKY, DON'T WALK ON THOSE MAGAZINES! THEY'RE HANGING OFF OF THE EDGE OF THE COFFEE TA-

whump!

YOU OK?

HEY, I'M *FABULOUS*. I'M JUST RESTING.

IS IT BAD THAT I THOUGHT THAT WAS FUNNY?

GOSH I LOVE ICE CREAM... IF I NEEDED A JOB, I WOULD START MY OWN ICE CREAM MAKING THINGY...

YOU COULD TEAM UP WITH A PIG AND CALL YOUR COMPANY "HOG AND DOG'S"

I DON'T GET IT.

UNFORTUNATELY I DO.

CHEWIN' ON FLEAS, EH? GOOD STUFF. JUST BE GLAD YOU DON'T HAVE THEM *SOUTH AMERICAN BEAVER FLEAS*... 8 MILLIMETERS LONG, I KID YOU NOT.

WHAT ARE YOU, THE *PETER GAMMONS* OF FLEAS?

WHO IS THIS *PETER GAMMONS* OF WHICH YOU SPEAK?

HE'S A WRITER. HE'S BASICALLY THE EXPERT ON BASEBALL.

WELL...MAYBE THIS *PETER GAMMONS* IS THE *BUCKY KATT* OF BASEBALL. EVER THOUGHT OF THAT?

I CAN HONESTLY SAY I'VE NEVER THOUGHT OF THAT.

WHAT ARE YOU WORKING ON? CAN WE HELP?

MY AGENCY IS WORKING ON A TOURISM CAMPAIGN FOR VERMONT. I'M WORKING ON A NEW STATE SLOGAN. IT NEEDS TO BE TRUTHFUL AND INFORMATIVE, BUT SORT OF FUNNY, TOO...

VERMONT: WHERE EVEN THE REDNECKS DRIVE "VOLVOS."

I CAN'T USE THAT.

HA HA HA! "VOLVO"! YOU MADE THAT UP!

OHH, THIS MOVIE IS SO BORING. PEOPLE ARE SO BORING... MOVIES SHOULDN'T HAVE PEOPLE IN THEM.

EXCUSE ME?

IN MY OPINION, THERE SHOULD BE MOVIES PRODUCED BY OTHER GROUPS. EVEN DOGS, IF THEY CAN FIGURE OUT HOW TO WORK THE CAMERA.

I MEAN, JUST PICTURE "INDIANA JONES" WITH ALL CATS!

AN ALL-CAT CAST? WHAT WOULD THAT BE, AN IN-ACTION MOVIE?

SEE, STARTING AN ALL-CAT MOVIE COMPANY WOULD SIMPLY BE THE FIRST STEP TO FORMING AN ALL-CAT SOCIETY. YES...I CAN PICTURE IT... A SECLUDED, TROPICAL ISLAND...FULL OF MILK STREAMS AND TUNA TREES...

WHOA... I DON'T EVEN WANT TO THINK ABOUT WHAT KIND OF WHACKO BANANA REPUBLIC THAT WOULD BE...

CAT REPUBLIC, ROB, HE'S TALKING ABOUT A CAT REPUBLIC...

I HAVE SEEN THE FUTURE, AND IT LICKS ITSELF CLEAN.

59

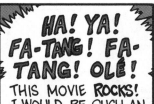

60

BUCKY, YOU **HAVE** TO STOP BITING SATCHEL...IF I THOUGHT IT WOULD HELP, I WOULD QUOTE "DO UNTO OTHERS AS YOU WOULD HAVE THEM DO UNTO YOU" - MATTHEW 7:12.

WELL, I WOULD RESPOND "DO UNTO CATS AND YOU'LL GET MESSED UP" - BUCKY.

7:45

SO YOU DO ADMIT THAT YOU BIT SATCHEL...

NO, NO, NO, I SAID I BIT "HIM." BUT IT ALL HAPPENED SO FAST, IT REALLY COULD HAVE BEEN **ANY** DOG.

BUCKY...

I MEAN, THEY ALL LOOK ALIKE, YOU KNOW?

WE DO NOT!

WAIT... I THOUGHT YOU SAID YOU BIT SATCHEL BECAUSE HE SNUCK UP BEHIND YOU...**HOW**, THEN, ARE YOUR TOOTH MARKS ON HIS **BACK**?

UM... YEAH, THAT WAS JUST FANG SHUI.

...YOU MEAN **FENG** SHUI? THIS I GOTTA HEAR.

YOU SEE...THE PRINCIPLES OF, UM, FLING SHUI ARE SO, UM, INBRED IN ME THAT EVEN THOUGH I WAS AMBUSHED, I HAD THE PRESENSE OF MIND TO BITE HIM IN THE MOST, UM, HARMONIOUS WAY.

"AMBUSH"? YOU FINISHED YOUR SNACK, DRANK SOME MILK, AND THEN YELLED "YOU'RE GOING DOWN POOCHY" BEFORE YOU BIT ME!

62

64

HI GUYS. I GOT A CAPPUCCINO MACHINE.

OH... OH. **OH!** THIS IS FANTASTIC. *FANTASTIC!*

CALM DOWN, DUDE, IT'S JUST A—

WHERE DO THE MONKEYS COME OUT OF IT?

...EXCUSE ME? "MONKEYS"? WHAT ON EARTH ARE YOU TALKING ABOUT?

DOES IT *MAKE* MONKEYS OR IS IT ONE OF THOSE ORGAN GRINDER THINGIES THE CAPPUCCINO MONKEYS COME *DANCE* TO?

WHAT THE?... HOLD ON, ARE YOU TALKING ABOUT *CAPUCHIN* MONKEYS? BUCKY, THIS IS A *CAPPUCCINO* MACHINE. IT MAKES *CAPPUCCINOS.*

MONKEYS IN *CHINOS?*

mmm.

69

GUYS, I LOST A LITTLE PHOTO... IT'S PART OF AN AD PROOF I NEED FOR WORK - HAVE YOU SEEN IT?

YEAH... I WANTED TO LOOK AT IT, BUT I WANTED TO EAT MY TAPIOCA, TOO, SO I PUT IT IN MY BOWL AND ATE AROUND IT.

ARE YOU TELLING ME THAT THAT'S MY AD PROOF STICKING OUT OF YOUR TAPIOCA?

THAT'S CORRECT.

HA HA HA! YOUR PROOF IS IN HIS PUDDING!

OK, PEOPLE, LISTEN UP. I LOST A VERY IMPORTANT BOOK. IF YOU **FIND** THIS BOOK, YOU ARE TO RETURN IT TO ME *IMMEDIATELY*. AND YOU ARE NOT - I REPEAT **NOT** - TO LOOK INSIDE IT. AND I FINALLY FIGURED OUT HOW TO OPEN THE FREEZER DOOR, SO YOU CAN'T HIDE STUFF FROM ME IN THERE ANYMORE.

HUNH... A GUY WHO'S *ONE-FOOT-EIGHT* LEARNED HOW TO OPEN THE FREEZER? THAT'S QUITE A TALENT HE PICKED UP THERE.

BUCKY KATT V.2.0. HEY, IT CAN'T BE MORE SCREWED UP THAN THE *BETA*.

AM I THE ONLY ONE WHO WONDERS WHAT THAT BOOK **IS**?

BUCK?... BUCKY, ARE YOU CRYING IN THERE? IS IT BECAUSE YOU LOST YOUR BOOK?... BUCK?

KNOCK KNOCK

I'M NOT CRYING! I DON'T CRY!

BUCK, YOU CRY EVERY TIME YOU LOSE SMACKY OR SPILL YOUR MILK... DUDE, YOU CRY MORE THAN A FRENCH SOCCER PLAYER.

HA HA HA! THAT'S FUNNY BECAUSE IT'S SO IMPOSSIBLE!

I THINK I FOUND BUCKY'S LOST BOOK!

REALLY? LET'S SEE.

HOLY COW - IT'S A **DIARY**..."JUNE 14: AS IS REQUIRED WHEN MY DINNER IS LATE, I TORE UP THE COUCH...JUNE 15: I WENT INTO THE LIVING ROOM WHERE THE GUY AND THE DOG WERE WATCHING TV AND STARED AT A BLANK WALL TO FREAK THEM OUT..."

HE DID! HE **DID** FREAK ME OUT!

HE ACTUALLY *RECORDS* HIS MOTIVATIONS FOR BEING ODD? SATCHEL, DO YOU REALIZE HOW IMPORTANT THIS IS?! IT'S LIKE THE *ROSETTA STONE* FOR CATS!

BUCKY? IS THIS THE BOOK YOU LOST?

MY... MY **DIARY!** YOU FOUND IT!

HIGH FOUR!

AAAA! DON'T HIT ME! I DIDN'T READ IT!

READING THAT BOOK ON SPOOKY, UNEXPLAINED STUFF, EH?

IT'S *INCREDIBLE!* THIS CHAPTER IS ABOUT A BABY WHO WAS BORN IN 1953 IN CALGARY ALREADY ABLE TO SPEAK *SWEDISH!*

AW, SATCH, YOU KNOW ALL THAT STUFF IS *FAKE*, RIGHT? IT'S LIKE *UFO's.*

WHAT-EFFOS?

UFO's.

I THINK HE MEANS *UNEXPLAINED FOUL ODORS.*

OHH! I'VE EXPERIENCED THOSE!

72

WHAT HAPPENED TO MY SHOES, BUCK? I LEFT THEM RIGHT HERE...

I MADE THEM DISAPPEAR. I'M MAGIC. I'M HARRY POTTER.

MAGIC ISN'T REAL, BUCK. AND "HARRY POTTER" IS FICTITIOUS.

NO, NO, HE'S BRITISH...

HARRY POTTER DOESN'T EXIST, BUCK. AND ANYWAY, YOU'RE NOT HIM.

I'M JUST LIKE HIM, THOUGH.

YEAH, HE'S HAIRY POTTER!

WAIT... "HARRY POTTER" IS... IS FICTITIOUS? BUT... BUT...

SATCH, IT'S A BOOK. IT'S MADE-UP... A WOMAN WROTE IT...

I... I DON'T THINK I CAN DEAL WITH THIS RIGHT NOW...

TRY GOING TO YOUR HAPPY PLACE, SATCH. THAT ALWAYS HELPS.

YES... YES, MY HAPPY PLACE... I... I SEE BAGS OF JERKY BITS...

HEYYY, JERKY BITS! GIVE ME—

BUCKY! YOU LEAVE HIM ALONE IN HIS HAPPY PLACE!

DUDE, I'M RENAMING YOU "CHICAGO"... THE WINDY KITTY.

ROB, ROB, ROB. I KEEP TELLING YOU - EVERYTHING ABOUT ME IS POWERFUL.

74

HI, GUYS, I'M HOME!

I WAS GETTING MY PIGGY BANK DOWN FROM THE SHELF AND BUCKY WAS STANDING RIGHT BEHIND ME BUT I DIDN'T KNOW IT AND I TURNED AROUND AND KNOCKED HIM OVER AND HE FELL AND PIGGY BROKE ON HIS HEAD AND HE WAS REALLY MAD AT ME BUT I DIDN'T MEAN TO—

SATCHEL, SATCHEL, SATCHEL, CALM DOWN... IT WAS AN ACCIDENT... BUCKY WILL HAVE FORGOTTEN ALL ABOUT THIS BY TOMORROW.

sniff

HE ALSO ATE TWO OF MY DIMES... *sniff* ...AND A NICKEL.

THEY TOO, SHALL PASS...

SEE, BUCK, THAT WAS WRONG TO EAT SATCHEL'S MONEY BECAUSE YOU WERE MAD AT HIM... AMONG *OTHER* REASONS...

ROBERT, I WAS PROVOKED.

NO, SEE, HIS DROPPING THE PIGGY BANK ON YOU WAS AN *ACCIDENT*. YOUR EATING HIS MONEY WAS ON *PURPOSE*...IN A WEIRD WAY, IT'S STEALING.

I...I WAS *ROBBED*?

TECHNICALLY YOU WERE *BUCKY-ED*.

OH... THAT'S *WORSE*, ISN'T IT?

HEY... WHAT ARE YOU DOING?

I'M GIVING SATCHEL A $10 ADVANCE ON HIS ALLOWANCE.

MAN! YOU NEVER GIVE *ME* 10 BUCKS!

I'M JUST GIVING IT TO GREENPEACE TO HELP THE WHALES.

YEAH, BUCK, YOU'D JUST BLOW IT ON CATNIP.

HEY, I CAN QUIT THE 'NIP ANY TIME I WANT.

76

I'M THINKING OF STARTING A LEMONADE STAND OUT IN THE HALLWAY. I FIGURE I'LL HAVE A MONOPOLY ON THE 4th-FLOOR FOOT TRAFFIC.

I DON'T KNOW, BUCK, THE HALL—

HEY, I THINK IT'S A GREAT IDEA. I DON'T NEED YOUR *VALIDATION.*

OK...SO...WHY ARE YOU STILL STANDING THERE?

WELL... I DO NEED YOUR MONEY.

WOULD YOU LIKE TO TRY A COMPLIMENTARY GLASS OF THE LEMONADE I'LL BE SELLING?

EUGH... IT LOOKS VILE. DID YOU USE *LEMONS*?

YES. FRESH OUT OF THE CAN.

LEMONS DON'T COME IN *CANS*, BUCKY.

SURE THEY DO... THE *FUZZY* ONES... FROM THE HALL CLOSET.

"FUZZY"? "HALL..."? DUDE, YOU LIQUIFIED TENNIS BALLS.

HEY! I BET THAT'S WHY THE BLENDER CAUGHT ON FIRE!

HOW'S THE LEMONADE RACKET IN THE FOURTH FLOOR HALLWAY, BUCK?

THE PRODUCT ISN'T MOVING QUITE AS WELL AS MY PRELIMINARY ANALYSIS PREDICTED.

TOMATOES
Lem

BUCKY, YOU ONLY ASKED *ONE PERSON* IF THEY WOULD BUY LEMONADE IN THE HALL, AND IT WAS *SATCHEL.*

...WHICH MEANS MY SAMPLING WAS 100% POSITIVE!

AND SURE ENOUGH, I BOUGHT ONE!

TOMATOES
Lem Lemonad

BUCK, I DON'T *DISLIKE* THE TASTE OF MEAT— I DON'T EAT OTHER ANIMALS BECAUSE I THINK THE WAY IT'S DONE IS *MEAN*.

WELL, THAT'S WHERE YOU'RE WRONG, PINKY. YOU *HAVE* TO EAT THEM TO SHOW THEM WHO'S *BOSS*. IF *EVERYBODY* STOPPED EATING COWS, THEY'D *TAKE OVER*, MAN! PRETTY SOON, YOU'D HAVE SOME BIG, JERKY COW RIGHT UP IN YOUR FACE SAYING *"DO MY LAUNDRY."*

COWS DON'T HAVE *LAUNDRY*, BUCK.

OH, THEY WILL... THEY WILL...

BUCKY... COWS WILL NOT *"TAKE OVER THE WORLD"* IF WE STOP EATING THEM.

IT'S NOT JUST *COWS*, MAN! IT'S *ALL* OF THE UPPITY ANIMALS WE EAT! YOU HAVE TO EAT *SOME* OF THEM TO KEEP THE OTHERS' EGOS IN CHECK! OTHERWISE, THEY'LL JUST BE UP IN OUR FACE ALL THE TIME!

SO... WHAT YOU'RE SAYING IS THAT I SHOULD OBJECT TO IGNORANT LITTLE CREATURES IMPOSING THEIR RIDICULOUS WILL ON ME, EH?

EXACTLY.

WATCH ME SINK THIS SHOT...

NOONAN! **NOONAN**! *NNNNOONAN*!

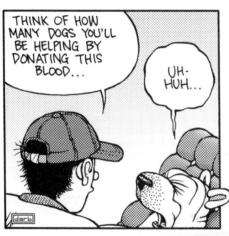

THE FOLLOWING ARE WORDS AND/OR PHRASES THAT I NEVER WANT TO HEAR IN THIS HOUSE AGAIN...

"COLLECTIBLE." "SHE'S GOOD PEOPLE." "PERSONAL DIGITAL ASSISTANT." "HE WENT YARD."

HE'S A SMALL, DRY-ROASTED **NUT**.

NOW WHY WOULD HE LEAVE "CARROT TOP" OFF THAT LIST?

LET'S GO, GUYS— WE'RE DRIVING MY DAD TO THE MEMORIAL SERVICE HELD BY THE RETIRED FIRE-FIGHTERS.

YOU LOOK SAD... ARE YOU SAD? YOU WANT YOUR HAT? WOULD THAT HELP?

YEAH.

...NNNNNHHHHH...

WHERE IS IT WHERE IS IT WHERE IS IT

AHHH!

SLURP
SLURP

THIS IS YOUR BRAIN ON CHEW TOYS.

BEHOLD! I, BUCKY KATT, HAVE CREATED THE NEWEST MEGA-HUGE TOY CRAZE OF THE MILLENNIUM... I GIVE YOU...

THE SKWUCKY!

SATCHEL...LISTEN... CRICKETS...

WHY IS THAT THING CALLED A "SKWUCKY"?

I COMBINED "BUCKY" AND "SQUARE"... AND I'M TELLIN' YA— IT'S GONNA BE HUGE WITH THE KIDS.

WHY WOULD A KID WANT A CARDBOARD SQUARE?

I'M BILLING IT AS AN EXCITING NEW CONCEPT IN "TOY".

...IT'S A SQUARE.

CORRECTION: IT'S A SKWUCKY.

IT WOULD BE SAFER IF IT WAS A BIRCLE.

BUCKY, YOU'RE NOT GONNA MAKE MONEY ON THAT. NO KID WANTS TO PLAY WITH A CARDBOARD SQUARE.

OH, OF COURSE THEY DO. *EVERYBODY* LOVES SQUARES. THEY'RE *INHERENTLY* EXCITING.

BUT WHAT DOES IT DO?

IT, UM... WELL... IT...

IT *ROCKS*. THAT'S WHAT IT DOES.

AW, YOU'RE MORE NUTS THAN A SQUIRREL PANTRY.

HA HA! I BET THEY HAVE **BIG** PANTRIES, TOO!

LISTEN, YOU CAN'T MAKE MONEY BY SLAPPING SOME PAINT ON A PIECE OF CARDBOARD AND SELLING IT AS A **TOY**... IT... HOLD ON... LET ME SEE THAT.

AAAA! THIS IS MY DAD'S 30-YEAR-OLD BEATLES ALBUM! YOU *PAINTED* IT! YOU PAINTED IT *RED*!

IT NEEDED TO BE EYE-CATCHING. IT WAS JUST PLAIN WHITE BEFORE.

IT'S THE *WHITE ALBUM*!

NOT ANYMORE!

I DON'T SEE WHY I'M *STILL* BEING PUNISHED FOR SPRAY-PAINTING A SILLY, OLD *"BEATLES"* ALBUM...

YOU NEED TO LET YOUR ANGER GO, ROBERT WILCO. THAT WAS *THEN* – THIS IS *NOW*... STOP LIVING IN THE PAST, MAN!

BUCKY, IT WAS FIVE MINUTES AGO.

I REMEMBER IT SO VIVIDLY...

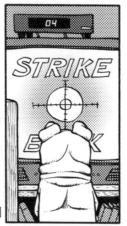

ROB! ROB! ROB! I WAS JUST OUTSIDE AND—

BUCKY, I'M WORKING HERE, AND YOU'RE NOT ALLOWED OUTSIDE, SO I DON'T WANT TO HEAR IT.

BUT ROB, SATCH—

YEAH, WHERE IS THAT GUY? HE WAS SUPPOSED TO BRING ME THE NEWSPAPER LIKE HALF AN HOUR AGO.

I'M *TRYING* TO TELL YOU! HE'S ON THE SIDEWALK, BLEEDING!

SATCHEL! ARE YOU OK? WHAT HAPPENED?

I... I THINK I'M OK... I CHASED A BICYCLE AND MY PAW GOT CAUGHT IN IT...

YOU CHASED A BIKE?! YOU HAVEN'T DONE THAT IN YEARS!

INDEED, IT WAS A VICIOUS CYCLE.

I CAN'T BELIEVE YOU CHASED A BIKE... *YOU*...

I SAW IT GOING BY AND I JUST SNAPPED... I COULDN'T CONTROL IT... I JUST NEEDED TO CATCH IT.

YOU KNOW, YOU'RE LUCKY THOSE SPOKES DIDN'T TAKE YOUR PAW OFF...

I MEAN, *HOW DO THEY MOVE?!* BIKES ARE SO *WEIRD!* THEY JUST GLIDE ALONG LIKE *SNAKES! I DON'T GET IT!* OK, STAY CALM, STAY CALM...

WELL, IT'S NOT AS BAD AS I THOUGHT, BUT YOU STILL HAVE TO BE SEEN.

YOU CAN'T SEE ME?!

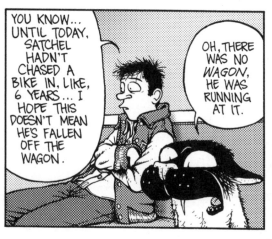

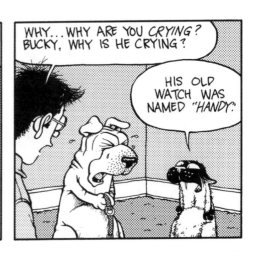

104

BUCKY, I JUST RAN INTO MRS. GARCIA IN THE HALL...

HOW FUN!

SHE MENTIONED THAT A VOODOO DOLL OF THEIR FERRET WAS PUSHED THROUGH THEIR PET FLAP TODAY... NATURALLY, SQUIGGLY CONSIDERED IT A THREAT...

NOW, SEE, I WOULD CONSIDER A *BUCKY DOLL* A *PRESENT*... I GUESS IT'S A FINE LINE, HUH?

IT'S A BIG, FAT, GLOW-IN-THE-DARK LINE!

IT SOUNDS PRETTY!

THEY'RE BAD ENOUGH STANDING THERE IN A DARK ALLEYWAY... BUT IT'S WHEN THEY *GLIDE BY YOU...* THAT THEY'RE THE WORST...

THE WEIRD SOUNDS... THE CHAINS... AND *HOW DO THEY MOVE?* IT'S SO *UNNATURAL!* FOR THE LOVE OF—

SATCHEL! I JUST NEED TO KNOW IF YOU COULD HANDLE ME BUYING THIS *STATIONARY BIKE* FOR EXERCISE!

OH, IT DOESN'T ACTUALLY MOVE? YEAH, IT SHOULD BE OK.

FREAK.

THAT'S DOG PROPAGANDA AND YOU KNOW IT.

NO, I'M SERIOUS... FOR EXAMPLE, WHO'S MY FAVORITE OF YOUR LITTLE CAT BUDDIES?

PROBABLY OATMEAL.

EXACTLY. AND *WHY?* BECAUSE HE'S FRIENDLY... SOCIAL... HE ANSWERS WHEN YOU CALL HIM...

HE EVEN SMELLS LESS "FISHY."

FACE IT, BUCK, MOST PEOPLE'S FAVORITE CATS ARE THE ONES WHO ACT LIKE *DOGS*.

LA! LA! LA! LA! I CAN'T HEAR YOU!

SO YOU'VE BEEN BUSY LATELY, BUCK...FINDING AND FIXING WATCHES...TAKING ON THE DUMPSTER RATS... PROVIDING YOUR OWN MEALS...YOU'RE ONE HAPPENIN' CAT.

WHAT CAN I SAY? I'M ON A ROLL.

REALLY? OH, WHOOPS, I'M ON A MUFFIN.

I'M GLAD TO GET THIS BANDAGE OFF, BUT I'M SAD TO LOSE MY SIGNATURES.

YOU HAVE SIGNATURES ON A CLOTH BANDAGE? WHERE?

SEE... THERE'S ONE RIGHT THERE.

OH YEAH... LET'S SEE..."SATCHEL"? WAIT, YOU SIGNED YOUR OWN NAME?

WELL... I REALLY DON'T GET OUT MUCH.

DUDE, YOU SIGNED YOUR OWN ARM, LIKE, SIX TIMES.

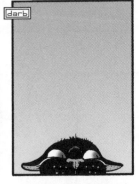

READY, BUD? IT'S TIME TO TAKE OFF YOUR BANDAGE.

I'VE BEEN READY FOR A MONTH!

OOF... IT'S KINDA FUNKY...

REALLY? I'M FUNKY?

POOCHY GOT DA **BAD** FUNK.

WOW...IT SMELLS LIKE SAUERKRAUT, DUDE...

HM. I THINK I WOULD LIKE SAUERKRAUT, THEN.

THAT SMELL IS GONNA RUIN MY ENTIRE DAY.

GET YOUR COLLARS, BOYS, WE'RE GOING OUT!

ALRIGHT! "OUT"!

WE'RE GOING TO SEE THE NUTCRACKER

OHHH, I DON'T LIKE VIOLENCE.

IF YOU'RE TAKING US TO THE VET, JUST SAY "THE VET."

SO WE HAVE TO RETURN BUCKY'S GIFT AND GET A NEW ONE, HUH? WHAT SHOULD WE GET?

THINK OF THINGS HE NEEDS.

OH! I KNOW! YOU KNOW THOSE TOWELS THAT SAY "MONDAY," "TUESDAY," "FRIDAY" ON THEM?

YEAH...

WE COULD GET HIM LITTLE TOWELS THAT SAY "2002," "2003," "2004."

I WANT HIM TO BATHE MORE THAN ONCE A YEAR, MAN.

125

127

HEY... WHERE ARE YOU GOING WITH MY BEANBAG?

MY FISH NEEDS A PLACE TO SLEEP.

BUT...BUT *I* SLEEP THERE... AND I SIT THERE ALL THE TIME... I WAS GOING THERE NOW...

OTHER PEOPLE HAVE NEEDS, TOO, SATCHEL!

BUT I HAD IT SHAPED JUST THE WAY I LIKED IT... IT'S SPECIFICALLY ADAPTED TO MY SHAPE...

I THINK WE'LL BE ABLE TO MIMIC "PEAR".

WHY DO YOU NEED ME TO GET YOUR BEANBAG FROM BUCKY? WHY DOES HE **HAVE** IT?

HE TOOK IT TO PUT HIS DEAD FISH ON.

HE...?... AND YOU *GAVE* IT TO HIM?

YOU KNOW I DON'T LIKE CONFLICT!

AW, SATCHEL! WHAT ARE YOU, **FRENCH**? YOU CAN'T JUST LAY DOWN LIKE THAT! YOU GOTTA STAND UP FOR YOURSELF!

...BUT THE FRENCH MODEL SEEMS TO SHOW THAT, ULTIMATELY, SOMEONE WILL DO MY WORK *FOR* ME...

Famous Cat Quotes

Darby Conley

Please Tell Dylan Thomas I'm very sorry.

DO NOT GO GENTLE INTO THAT COLD BATH!

ARE YA HAPPY? I'M BLEEDING!

128